Battle of the Ironclads

by Michael Burgan

Content Adviser: Paul Christopher Anderson, Ph.D.,
Associate Professor, Department of History,
Clemson University

Reading Adviser: Susan Kesselring, M.A.,
Literacy Educator,
Rosemount–Apple Valley–Eagan (Minnesota) School District

COMPASS POINT BOOKS
MINNEAPOLIS, MINNESOTA

Compass Point Books
3109 West 50th Street, #115
Minneapolis, MN 55410

Visit Compass Point Books on the Internet at *www.compasspointbooks.com*
or e-mail your request to *custserv@compasspointbooks.com*

On the cover: An 1891 oil painting by J.G. Tanner of the engagement between the *Monitor* and
the *Virginia* (formerly the *Merrimack*)

Photographs ©: The Granger Collection, New York, cover, 5, 37; Prints Old and Rare, back
cover (far left); Library of Congress, back cover, 11, 12, 21, 22, 25, 31, 41; North Wind Picture
Archives, 4, 13, 15, 23, 24, 26, 27, 29, 40; Corbis, 7, 34, 39; Archivo Iconografico, S.A./Corbis,
9; Mary Evans Picture Library, 10; U.S. Naval Historical Center, 16, 20, 28, 35, 36, 38; William
Bardsley/Hulton Archive/Getty Images, 18; The Mariners' Museum, Newport News, Va., 19;
Medford Historical Society Collection/Corbis, 32; Time Life Pictures/National Archives/Getty
Images, 33.

Managing Editor: Catherine Neitge
Page Production: Bobbie Nuytten
Photo Researcher: Marcie C. Spence
Cartographer: XNR Productions, Inc.
Library Consultant: Kathleen Baxter

Creative Director: Keith Griffin
Editorial Director: Carol Jones

Library of Congress Cataloging-in-Publication Data
Burgan, Michael.
  The battle of the ironclads / by Michael Burgan.
     p. cm.—(We the people)
  Includes bibliographical references and index.
  ISBN 0-7565-1628-5 (hard cover : alk. paper)
  ISBN 0-7565-1768-0 (paperback)
  1. Hampton Roads, Battle of, Va., 1862—Juvenile literature. 2. Monitor (Ironclad)—Juvenile
literature. 3. Virginia (Ironclad)—Juvenile literature. 4. Merrimack (Frigate)—Juvenile literature. 5.
United States—History—Civil War, 1861–1865—Naval operations—Juvenile literature. 6. Virginia—
History—Civil War, 1861-1865—Naval operations—Juvenile literature. I. Title. II.
We the people (Series) (Compass Point Books)
  E473.2.B87 2006
  973.7'52—dc22   2005025080

TABLE OF CONTENTS

A HISTORIC BATTLE

The wooden ship *Minnesota* sat motionless in the water at Hampton Roads, Virginia. The day before, on March 8, 1862, the *Minnesota* and several other Union Navy ships had been badly damaged. Most of the damage had been done by the Confederate ironclad *Virginia,* formerly called the *Merrimack.* The *Virginia* had thick iron plates over a wooden frame. Cannonballs fired

Sailors swim for their lives after their Union ship, the Congress, *was attacked by the* Virginia.

4

from the Union ships bounced off the *Virginia's* sides like hail bouncing off a window. At the same time, the wooden ships had no defense against the exploding shells fired from the ironclad's guns.

The fighting at Hampton Roads was one of the first major naval battles of the Civil War, the four-year con-flict between the Confederacy and the Union. The Confederacy was formed when 11 states from the South seceded, or left the United States. The Confederate states allowed slavery and believed President

President Abraham Lincoln

Abraham Lincoln would take away their citizens' right to own slaves. They thought forming their own nation was the only way to protect that right. Lincoln fought the Civil War to keep the Southern states in the Union.

Now, on the morning of March 9, the *Virginia* prepared to destroy the already damaged *Minnesota*. But as the ironclad approached its enemy, the Confederate sailors saw a strange new ship in the water. During the night, a Union ironclad called the *Monitor* had reached Hampton Roads.

The *Monitor* was flat, with most of the ship under the surface of the water. In the middle sat a turret, which held the ironclad's two large guns. The Southerners called the *Monitor* "an immense shingle floating in the water" and "a cheesebox on a tray." The Union ironclad was much smaller than the *Virginia,* and at first the Confederate sailors did not notice its guns. Almost everyone who saw the *Monitor*—including Union sailors on the *Minnesota*—thought the odd ironclad would never survive.

When the fighting began, however, the *Monitor*

Most of the Union ironclad Monitor *was under the water.*

proved just as tough as the *Virginia*. For almost four hours, the two ships fired at each other. Their battle was the first ever between two ironclads. One would eventually retreat, but naval warfare would never be the same again.

THE FIRST IRONCLADS

By the 1820s, several countries had guns on their ships that fired shells. Shells had replaced the solid iron balls, called shot, which had commonly been used on ships. Shipbuilders had learned how to build wooden ships strong enough to survive being hit by shot. But now they needed something new to protect against the explosions and fires caused by shells. Iron was the answer.

During the 1850s, the French built iron-covered wooden platforms called floating batteries. The platforms were towed into position in the water by ships. The platforms could get close to enemy forts near the water, since the enemy's shells could not damage them. In one battle, a French floating platform destroyed a fort without receiving any damage itself.

The next step was to build an actual iron ship, powered by steam engines and sails. Once again, the French took the lead. In 1859, they launched the *Gloire*. It was

8

The Crimean War in the 1850s saw the first use of iron-covered platforms.

85 yards (77 meters) long and had sides covered in iron almost 5 inches (12.7 centimeters) thick. The next year, Great Britain built its first iron warship, called the *Warrior*.

At this time, the United States was not interested in building ironclads. It had a small navy compared to Great Britain and France, and its ships rarely went to battle.

Great Britain's iron warship, the Warrior

But a Florida lawmaker named Stephen Mallory had studied U.S. naval affairs in the 1850s and knew what Europeans were building. He tried to convince U.S. officials that the country should build its own iron-covered floating battery. Mallory failed, but he soon had a chance to actually build an ironclad ship.

Florida was one of the Southern states that formed the Confederacy. In March 1861, Mallory was put in

charge of the new Confederate
Navy. Just a little more
than a month later,
the Civil War began,
and Mallory thought
about ironclad ships.

He wrote,
"Such a vessel …
could [travel] the
entire coast of the
United States … and
encounter, with a fair pros-
pect of success, their entire Navy."

Stephen Mallory

He wanted to buy a ship like the *Gloire* or *Warrior*.
Neither France nor Great Britain, however, wanted to sell
their powerful warships. They did not want to appear to
favor the South over the North. Mallory realized that the
Confederacy would have to build its own ironclads.

LOSS OF THE *MERRIMACK*

In the weeks before the Civil War, the United States hoped to protect its naval property in Southern ports. Virginia was a Southern state that seemed likely to secede. It was also the home of the Gosport Navy Yard. Located in Portsmouth, near Norfolk, Gosport was the largest shipyard in the country. Gideon Welles, secretary of the U.S. Navy, feared that the United States could not defend the shipyard if it came under Southern attack. He made plans to move ships out of the yard as soon as possible. The most important of these ships was the *Merrimack*.

The United States had built the *Merrimack* in 1856.

Gideon Welles

The USS Merrimack *was named for the Merrimack River.*

It was one of the biggest ships in the Navy and it carried 40 large guns. The *Merrimack* used both steam engines and sails for power. Its coal-burning steam engines, however, often broke down. In April 1861, the *Merrimack* was at Gosport for repairs. On April 11, Welles ordered the *Merrimack* moved to Philadelphia. Before the ship could leave, however, the Civil War began.

13

The following week, Virginia seceded from the Union. Welles sent an order to Charles McPauley, the commander at the shipyard, telling him not to let the Confederates take the ships and weapons there. Welles added, "Should it finally become necessary, you will, in order to prevent that result, destroy the property."

Most of the workers and sailors at the shipyard were Southerners, and they joined the Confederacy. No one was left to get the ships out of the harbor. McPauley feared that Southern troops were on their way to Gosport. Following Welles' order, he told the remaining men to destroy the ships and the docks. Sailors sank the *Merrimack* and then set it on fire. The flames burned the top part of the hull, but the rest settled into the Elizabeth River.

On April 21, Confederate forces entered Gosport. They found what was left of the *Merrimack*. They raised the damaged hull out of the water and found the engines. The men saw that much of the ship could be used again. Stephen Mallory was already working with several engi-

Union soldiers set fire to the Merrimack *and the shipyard.*

neers on building an ironclad. They realized the quickest way to build one was to use the remains of the *Merrimack*. In July, the Confederacy began building its new warship, which they renamed the *Virginia*. For much of the war, and even to this day, however, most people still called it the *Merrimack*.

BUILDING THE IRONCLADS

Through spies, Gideon Welles heard about the Confederacy's work with the *Merrimack*. He decided the Union needed its own ironclad ships. The first design the Navy approved looked like the British and French models. The ironclad was basically a wooden sailing ship with an iron hull. It also had steam engines to help provide power.

Then Welles saw a design for a new kind of warship. It was made by John Ericsson, a Swedish inventor living in the United States.

The Monitor *was based on John Ericsson's design.*

Ericsson's ironclad looked nothing like the ironclads of Europe. He saw it as a floating battery that could move under its own steam power. The ship was flat, like a raft, except for its gun turret. Some naval officials doubted that Ericsson's design would work. Still, the Navy took a risk and used his plan for the new ironclad. That ship became the *Monitor*.

At the same time, the Confederacy was continuing its work on the *Merrimack*. It now looked much different from existing European ironclads and wooden ships. The original plan for the ship was drawn by several men, including John Luke Porter and John Mercer Brooke. Porter was a ship designer, and Brooke was a Confederate naval officer and inventor.

The two men designed an ironclad with a large covered area, called a casement, with sloped sides. The ship's cannons were in the casement, which sat on top of a long hull—in this case, the one from the *Merrimack*. Brooke wanted a regular ship's hull so the ironclad could

The crew of the Monitor *on the deck of the Union ironclad*

sail almost as quickly as a wooden ship could. The hull sat completely underwater. As Brooke wrote, "Nothing was to be seen afloat but the shield itself."

Both the North and the South designed their ironclads to be powerful warships. The men who eventually sailed them, however, faced difficult living conditions. The ships' iron held in heat during the summer and allowed in cold during the winter. The sailors lived in damp, crowded spaces. Gases from the ships' engines made breathing hard.

18

MISSION OF THE *MONITOR*

The Confederacy had a head start in the race to build an ironclad. But problems slowed down the process. The South lacked good railways, and shipping hundreds of tons of iron to Gosport was difficult. Meanwhile, the North moved quickly to build its ironclad. Ericsson's ship was much smaller than the *Merrimack*, and the North had greater supplies of iron. Union shipbuilders in New York had the *Monitor* in the water by the end of January 1862.

The Monitor *was launched from New York's Continental Iron Works in January 1862.*

19

The ship, however, was still not complete, and it had to go through several tests at sea.

At first, the tests did not go well. Because of trouble with the steam engine, the *Monitor* sailed more slowly than expected. Newspaper reporters who saw the test made fun of Ericsson, but he soon fixed the problem. A few days later, a problem with the steering forced the ship to return to port. Finally on March 6, the *Monitor* left New York and headed for Virginia. Another Navy ship towed it, and the *Monitor* used its own engine power as well.

An illustration of the Monitor *appeared in* Harper's Weekly *in March 1862.*

The ironclad's mission was to confront the *Virginia* and prevent it from destroying the ships at Hampton Roads. Although Virginia was a Confederate state, the Union controlled the land north of Hampton Roads and Norfolk. Union ships sat in the nearby James River, and Union soldiers also manned batteries on the shore.

John Worden commanded the *Monitor*. The captain and his crew of 57 almost did not reach Virginia. On the *Monitor*'s second day on the Atlantic Ocean, a fierce storm hit, causing rough seas. Water began to leak into the ship. One officer wrote that "the water came down under the turret like a waterfall." For a time, the fans designed to bring fresh air

Captain John Worden

21

into the ship shut off and the engine stopped. Some sailors fainted from breathing stale air. The *Monitor* bobbed in the crashing waves, and some of the crew feared for their lives. Finally, the ship that was towing the *Monitor* managed to pull it closer to shore, where the sea was calmer.

While the *Monitor* was fighting for survival, the Confederates were finishing up the *Virginia*. The ironclad had 10 guns in its casement and could carry a crew of about 300. The ship also had a large piece of iron in its bow that could be used to ram enemy ships. The commander of the *Virginia* was Captain Franklin Buchanan. He led a squadron of six ships that would attack Union ships in the area.

Captain Franklin Buchanan

THE *VIRGINIA* ATTACKS

On March 8, Buchanan ordered the shipyard workers off the *Virginia*. Unlike the Northerners, he was not going to test his ship before going into battle. He wanted the *Virginia* and the rest of his squadron to attack that day. As the *Virginia* sailed, Buchanan told his crew, "The whole world is watching you today." The *Virginia* and two smaller Navy boats headed for the mouth of the James River. One of the Union soldiers onshore who saw the *Virginia* approaching called it "a black, wicked looking craft."

As the *Virginia* steamed across Hampton Roads, several Union ships sat waiting. Between them, the

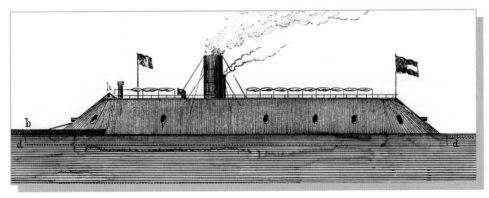

The Virginia *could shoot and ram enemy ships.*

23

The Virginia *rammed the Union ship, the* Cumberland.

Union ships had more than 200 large guns. They fired
at the *Virginia*, but the shots bounced off the ironclad.
The Confederate ship then sailed toward the Union ship
Congress. Southern shells tore through the wooden ship
and killed many sailors. Then the *Virginia* headed for the
Cumberland, a Union ship with several heavy guns. The
Southerners fired their guns, then Buchanan ordered his
ironclad to ram the Union ship. Soon water was flowing
into the *Cumberland*. The *Virginia's* iron ram broke off,
but it had done its job. The *Cumberland* sank into the harbor, and the ironclad began firing again at the *Congress*. A
Union captain on a nearby ship later wrote, "The blood

was running from the *Congress* … on to our decks." Within an hour, the Union ship surrendered.

From the shore, Union soldiers fired both cannons and rifles at the attacking ships. At one point, Buchanan went up on deck of the *Virginia*. A Union rifle shot hit him in the leg, and he was forced to give up command. Buchanan's last order was "to fight … as long as the men could stand to their guns." He turned the ship over to Commander Catesby ap Roger Jones.

Union troops fired at the Virginia *from the shore.*

A battlefield sketch of the Virginia *passing Confederate troops*

The *Virginia* headed next for the *Minnesota*. This Union ship had gotten trapped in mud in the harbor and could not move. Near it was the *St. Lawrence*, which was also aground. Luckily for the Union ships, the water near them was shallow. The *Virginia* was too large to get closer than 1 mile (1.6 kilometers), and its guns could not do much damage. Still, two small ships in Buchanan's squadron were able to move closer. Their guns badly damaged the *Minnesota*. As night fell, the Confederate squadron pulled away. The *Virginia* would return the next day to try to finish off the *Minnesota* and the other surviving Union ships.

26

THE IRONCLADS BATTLE

Off the coast of Virginia, the crew of the *Monitor* could see flashes of light and clouds of smoke from batteries and cannons. The Union ironclad, however, arrived at Hampton Roads too late to join the fight. That night, the *Monitor* sailed close to the *Minnesota* and waited for the *Virginia* to return. The next day, Captain Worden told the captain of the *Minnesota*, "I will stand by you to the last if I can help you." The *Minnesota's* officers, however, did not think the tiny *Monitor* could stop the powerful *Virginia*.

The little Monitor *arrives at Hampton Roads.*

27

Shortly before 8 A.M., the *Virginia* began to approach the *Minnesota*. At first, the Confederates ignored the new ship lying between it and the wooden Union ship. The *Virginia* fired at the damaged *Minnesota*, and the Union ship returned fire. Soon, however, the morning's main battle was between the two ironclads. The *Monitor* sailed closer to the *Virginia* and began its attack. The *Virginia* fired back its shells. One observer said the Confederates' shells "had no more effect, apparently, than so many pebblestones thrown by a child."

The Virginia *is flanked by the* Minnesota *(left) and the* Monitor.

The Union sailors needed seven minutes to load their two guns. The turret first turned away from the *Virginia*. Inside the hot turret, the men were covered with sweat and gunpowder. Once the guns were loaded, the turret turned back toward the target, and the guns fired. The guns, however, were not powerful enough to damage the *Virginia*.

Although the *Virginia* could reload faster, it had its own problems. Several of its guns had been damaged during the first day of fighting. And the commander had to turn the whole ship to aim his guns at the *Monitor*. The guns themselves could not turn, as the *Monitor*'s turret could. The *Monitor* was also faster and easier to move in the water than the *Virginia*. It could easily change its position

The Monitor's *guns were inside a turret.*

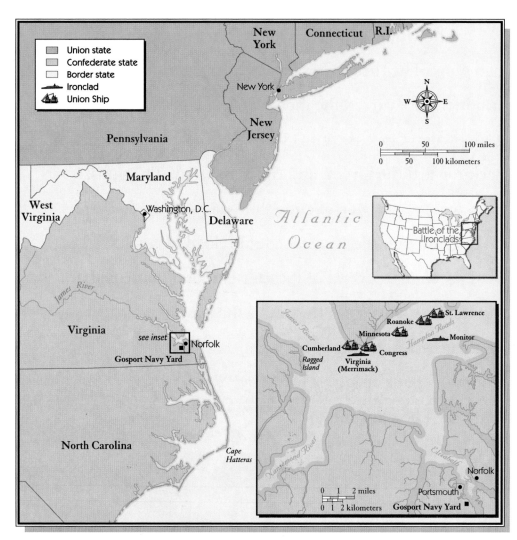

The ironclads faced off in Hampton Roads.

before the Confederates fired.

Jones saw that he could not damage the Northern ironclad. He then turned his guns back on the *Minnesota*.

As it moved closer, the *Virginia* ran aground. The crew in the engine room worked to create more power, so the ship could get off the ground. They threw wood, cotton, rags, and coal into the steam boilers that powered the engines.

A Confederate sailor later described the sounds he heard: "the cracking, roaring fire, escaping steam, and the loud, labored [noise] of the engines." Meanwhile, the *Monitor* sailed closer to the *Virginia*. Its two guns blasted at the Southern ironclad's casement. If the Confederate ship was aground too long, the Northern ironclad might begin to damage it. Finally, the *Virginia* was able to pull itself back into the water.

The Monitor *(left) clashed with the Confederate ironclad, the* Virginia.

As noon approached, neither ironclad had managed to damage the other. The worst blow of the day came when a Southern shell exploded in the *Monitor*'s pilothouse. At that moment, Worden was looking out a slot in the side of the ship. The explosion knocked off part of the roof of the pilothouse and wounded Worden in the eyes and face. He missed the rest of the battle, but told the officers, "I cannot see, but do not mind me. Save the *Minnesota* if you can."

The battle, however, was almost over. The *Virginia* had started to leak, and it still could not get close enough to the *Minnesota* to destroy it. Jones ordered the ship back to Gosport for repairs. The *Monitor* remained in Hampton Roads, ready to fight again if the *Virginia* returned.

W.N. Jeffers took command after Worden was hurt.

END OF THE TWO IRONCLADS

Onboard the *Monitor*, the crew thought it had won the battle of the ironclads. They had saved the *Minnesota*, as they had been ordered to do. The Confederates, however, saw the two-day battle as a major victory. The *Virginia* had destroyed two Union ships and badly damaged a third. The Southerners had also killed several hundred enemy sailors. No Confederate crew members had died during the fighting.

For several weeks, Southern ship workers repaired the *Virginia*. They put on a new iron ram, replaced the damaged guns, and

The Monitor's *turret armor had dents from hits by the Confederates' heavy guns.*

The Virginia *was one of 22 ironclads built by the Confederacy.*

added extra iron plates. The ship also received new shot designed to pierce the iron sides of the *Monitor*. Still, the Confederates did not think they could destroy the *Monitor* with gunfire. Instead, they had a new plan. The *Virginia* would fire at the *Monitor*, while smaller Confederate boats pulled up next to the Union ship. Then sailors from those boats would start fires inside the *Monitor* by dropping small bombs down its smokestack. Other sailors would jam pieces of metal into the turret so it could not turn.

As the Confederates made their plans, the North was

also at work. The Union had sent other ships to join the *Monitor* in Hampton Roads. They included another iron-clad and a ship with a huge ram. If the *Virginia* returned, the North hoped to sink it by ramming it. The North had heard about the South's plans for attacking the *Monitor*. Northern officers planned to keep their ironclads far from the *Virginia* and the small boats that traveled with it. Likewise, the South knew about the North's plans to ram the *Virginia*. It would also stay far away from danger.

Northern leaders counted on the *Monitor* to play a key role in a new attack. General George McClellan was

Union ships were in the area to support General George McClellan's troops.

bringing Union troops into Virginia through Hampton Roads by water. His men would advance along the James and York rivers to try to capture Richmond, the Confederate capital. McClellan hoped the *Monitor* could protect the wooden Union ships from attack by the *Virginia*.

On April 11, the *Virginia* left Gosport and sailed into Hampton Roads. Josiah Tattnall was now the ironclad's captain. He hoped to capture or sink the *Monitor*. But the Confederates could not draw the *Monitor* into a battle. Neither ironclad came close to the other. Neither one wanted to risk defeat. Both sides fired at each other from long range. None of the ships were hit.

36

The ironclads faced off, but avoided a battle in Hampton Roads on April 11, 1862.

By May, McClellan was having some success in his advance on Richmond. The Confederates decided to pull out of the Norfolk area. The *Virginia* was out of port when the Confederates left the Gosport Navy Yard.

Tattnall knew the *Virginia* could not safely return to its home port. It also

General George McClellan

could not sail past Union troops on the shore and reach the open sea. The land guns were much more powerful than the guns on Union ships. Tattnall decided to try to sail up the James River to reach the Confederate capital of Richmond. But first he had to lighten the ship, so it could sail in the river's shallow waters.

For hours, the *Virginia's* crew threw food, coal, and other supplies into the water. However, the ship was still too heavy to reach Richmond. And now it sat higher in the water than it was designed to and could be more easily hit by enemy fire. Tattnall knew it was too risky to take the ship into battle. And he did not want to leave the *Virginia* at Gosport so the Union could capture it. The Confederate captain decided to destroy the ship. First, he ran it aground on a small island. Then the crew set out a line of gunpowder that ran to the *Virginia's* main supply of gunpowder. They lit the line before leaving the ship. The fuse burned until it blew up the ship's 18 tons of gunpowder.

Captain Josiah Tattnall

On the *Monitor*, the crew heard a loud explosion. They guessed what had happened. By now, the Union sailors were calling the

The Confederates blew up the Virginia *so it would not be captured by Union forces.*

Virginia "the Big Thing." The sailors were disappointed the enemy had destroyed their own ship. An officer named William Keeler wrote, "We felt confident that she would die [fighting] rather than fall by her own hand."

The *Monitor* soon steamed into Norfolk. The ironclad stayed in Hampton Roads for most of the rest of the year. It briefly sailed up the James River, hoping to attack Richmond. Confederate batteries, however, forced it to turn around. The ship also spent time at a shipyard in Washington, D.C., before returning to Virginia.

On December 25, 1862, the *Monitor* was ordered to sail to North Carolina. While being towed at sea, it ran into a storm. One sailor later described the rough seas. The ship bounced up and down "with such force that her hull would tremble, and with a shock that would sometimes take us off our feet." Water began to pour in around the turret and between the upper and lower levels of the ship. The crew abandoned the *Monitor* and was picked up by the ship towing it. The ironclad was left to sink into the ocean.

Despite that loss, the Union Navy had great success

The USS Rhode Island *saved the crew of the* Monitor *as the ironclad sank in a gale.*

during the rest of the Civil War. The North had many more ships than the South and controlled the Atlantic Ocean and many rivers to the west. The North's powerful navy played a key role in winning the war.

Both the North and the South built new ironclads during the Civil War. But none of those ships ever won the fame of the *Monitor* and the *Virginia*. The world remembers their battle because it began a new age of warfare at sea. No major navy would ever again go to war with wooden ships.

The Union ironclad Montauk *followed the success of the* Monitor.

41

GLOSSARY

aground—stuck on land or on the bottom of a body of water

batteries—groups of large guns arranged in one spot

bow—the very front of a ship

Confederacy—the Southern states that fought against the Northern states in the Civil War; also called the Confederate States of America

hull—the frame or body of a ship

pilothouse—the room on a ship with the steering wheel

secretary—the head of a government department

shells—metal containers filled with gunpowder or metal and fired from a large gun

shipyard—the place where ships are built and repaired

turret—an enclosed, movable space that holds guns; a small tower on a building

Union—the United States of America; also the Northern states that fought against the Southern states in the Civil War

42

DID YOU KNOW?

- The battle of Hampton Roads is often called the battle of the *Monitor* and the *Merrimack* and not the battle of the *Monitor* and the *Virginia*. Northern newspapers and military officials always referred to the Confederate ironclad by its original name.

- Each shot fired from the *Monitor's* guns weighed 175 pounds (78.7 kilograms). More than 3 tons of iron shot was fired at the *Virginia* without damaging it.

- The *Monitor's* guns could not rise high enough to fire shot long distances through the air. The ship's guns had to skip the shot across the water toward the *Virginia*.

- In 1973, scientists found remains of the *Monitor* in the waters near Cape Hatteras, North Carolina. Divers have recovered the ship's anchor as well as other items, which are now on display at the Mariners' Museum in Newport News, Virginia.

- Today, the word *ironclad* has another meaning. People use it to describe anything that can't be easily destroyed or broken, such as an "ironclad agreement."

IMPORTANT DATES

Timeline

1856	The U.S. Navy builds the *Merrimack*.
1859	France builds the first ironclad warship.
1860	In December, the first of 11 Southern states secedes from the Union to form the Confederacy.
1861	In March, Stephen Mallory is put in charge of the Confederate Navy; in April, the Civil War begins, and the Confederates take over the Gosport Navy Yard; in July, work begins to turn the *Merrimack* into an ironclad, which is renamed the *Virginia*; in October, the Union begins to build the *Monitor*.
1862	In March, the *Monitor* almost sinks while sailing to Virginia; on March 8, the *Virginia* destroys two Union ships at Hampton Roads, Virginia; the next day, the *Monitor* and the *Virginia* fight the first battle between two ironclads; in May, the Confederates destroy the *Virginia* rather than risk losing it to the Union; in December, the *Monitor* sinks in rough waters off North Carolina.

IMPORTANT PEOPLE

JOHN MERCER BROOKE (1826–1906)
Confederate officer and inventor who helped design the Virginia

FRANKLIN BUCHANAN (1800–1874)
First commander of the Virginia *after it became an ironclad*

JOHN ERICSSON (1803–1889)
Inventor who designed the Monitor

CATESBY AP ROGER JONES (1821–1877)
Commander of the Virginia *during its battle with the* Monitor; *the "ap" in his name is a Welsh term indicating "son of;" therefore, he was Catesby, son of Roger, Jones*

JOHN LUKE PORTER (1813–1893)
Ship designer who helped create the ironclad Virginia

JOSIAH TATTNALL (1795–1871)
Last captain of the Virginia

JOHN WORDEN (1818–1897)
First captain of the Monitor

WANT TO KNOW MORE?

At the Library

Anderson, Dale. *The Civil War at Sea.* Milwaukee, Wis.: World Almanac
Library, 2004.

Brager, Bruce L. *The Monitor vs. the Merrimack.* Philadelphia: Chelsea
House Publishers, 2003.

McPherson, James M. *Fields of Fury: The American Civil War.* New York:
Atheneum Books for Young Readers, 2002.

O'Brien, Patrick. *Duel of the Ironclads: The Monitor vs. the Virginia.* New
York: Walker & Company, 2003.

Sheridan, Robert E. *Iron from the Deep: The Discovery and Recovery of the
USS Monitor.* Annapolis, Md.: Naval Institute Press, 2003.

On the Web

For more information on the *Battle of the Ironclads,* use FactHound
to track down Web sites related to this book.

1. Go to *www.facthound.com*

2. Type in a search word related to this book
   or this book ID: 0756516285

3. Click on the *Fetch It* button.

Your trusty FactHound will fetch the best Web sites for you!

On the Road

The Mariners' Museum
100 Museum Drive
Newport News, VA 23606
800/581-7245
Maritime museum that houses items
recovered from the *Monitor*

Trophy Park
Norfolk Naval Shipyard
Portsmouth, VA 23709
757/396-9551
Park located on a portion of the
original Gosport Navy Yard site that
displays weapons and artifacts from
the Civil War and other U.S. wars

Look for more We the People books about this era:

The Assassination of Abraham Lincoln
ISBN 0-7565-0678-6

The Battle of Gettysburg
ISBN 0-7565-0098-2

The Carpetbaggers
ISBN 0-7565-0834-7

The Emancipation Proclamation
ISBN 0-7565-0209-8

Fort Sumter
ISBN 0-7565-1629-3

The Gettysburg Address
ISBN 0-7565-1271-9

Great Women of the Civil War
ISBN 0-7565-0839-8

The Lincoln-Douglas Debates
ISBN 0-7565-1632-3

The Missouri Compromise
ISBN 0-7565-1634-X

The Reconstruction Amendments
ISBN 0-7565-1636-6

Surrender at Appomattox
ISBN 0-7565-1626-9

The Underground Railroad
ISBN 0-7565-0102-4

A complete list of We the People titles is available on our Web site:
www.compasspointbooks.com

INDEX

About the Author

Michael Burgan is a freelance writer of books for children and adults. A history graduate of the University of Connecticut, he has written more than 90 fiction and nonfiction children's books. For adult audiences, he has written news articles, essays, and plays. Michael Burgan is a recipient of an Educational Press Association of America award.